Hark! Follow My Hoofbeats

Mary Chris Foxworthy

Cover Art: Dana Bauer

Hark! Follow My Hoofbeats

More books from Hoofbeats Through History

Learn world history in a fun way - through the eyes of a horse!

No Man to Romans - Eocene Epoch to 476 AD
Dark to Light - 476 AD - 1250 AD
Armor to Art - 1250 AD - 1600 AD
Muddy Roads to Men on the Moon - 1600 AD - 1961 AD

Be sure to visit the website : www.hoofbeatsthroughhistory.com
The web site provides more information about horses and history.
Hark and his stablemates even have a blog on the site!

Even really smart horses need a little help writing a book so Hark's owner, Mary Chris Foxworthy, helped him. Mary Chris' grandfather owned one of the last creameries in the United States that still used horse-drawn milk wagons. This sparked her life-long love affair with horses and a passion for keeping horse history alive and led to work as a research writer for The Equine Heritage Institute. Mary Chris is also an active exhibitor in Carriage Driving and Dressage.

Dear Reader,

You might travel to and from school on a bus. When you go shopping or to visit family and friends you may get there by car. But as short as 150 years ago, you would be getting where you had to go with a horse.

I am a Morgan horse and my name is Hark. Horses have been an important part of human history from the very beginning! The path through history is paved with hoofprints.

I can't wait for you to travel through time with me and learn about amazing events, meet re-markable people and learn about the important contributions hors-es have made throughout history.

But first...how did I even get here? What did my ancient relatives look like? How did I come to be? That's what this book is all about. I hope you enjoy it!

Hark

TABLE OF CONTENTS

CHAPTER 1 ~ Only Horses

Over fifty-five million years ago my ancestors were here on earth. I am a horse and my name is HD Harkness - but you can call me Hark. This is a picture of me in my field. I'm a Morgan horse. My ancestors were here long before there were humans!

Humans have only been here about two hundred thousand years and civilization as we know it is only about six thousand years old.

I am a mammal and I am an herbivore. Over the time of fifty-five million years, there have been a few hundred, now extinct, species of the genus Equus. Today there are only seven species of Equus. My horse family today is quite small. All horse breeds, from slim thoroughbred racehorses to stocky plow horses to tiny ponies, belong to a single species, Equus caballus.

Long before there were breeds of horses like Morgans, horses looked different. The first horses did not look like me at all but over time, horses evolved into a large, four-legged animal that was ultimately domesticated by humans. Learn more about what early horses looked like here: https://www.britannica.com/animal/horse/Evolution-of-the-horse

Horses belong to a group of mammals with an odd number of toes. Mammals with two toes, or "cloven hooves", like goats, pigs, cows, deer and camels do not belong to my family.

My four-toed horse ancestor was very fast. He needed to be fast to evade predators. The middle toe developed into the hoof that I have now; over time it became bigger and better able to provide traction for a fast get-away. The other toes became smaller and eventually disappeared.

Horses now have three "toes" on each leg. Did you know that?! You can see my hoof and if you look closely, you can see the remains of the other two tiny, shrunken toes on the bones above each of my hoofs. These "toes" are called the ergots and the chestnuts.

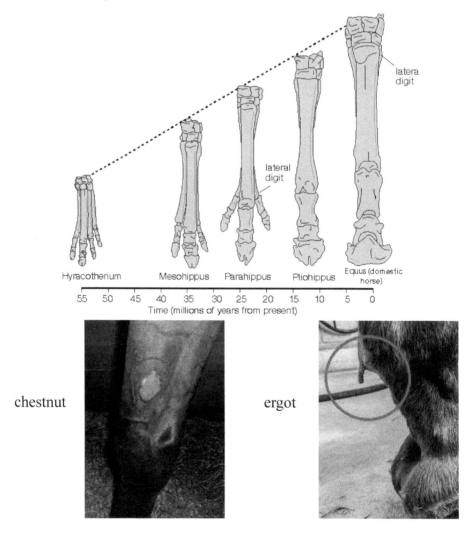

latera digit

lateral digit

Hyracotherium   Mesohippus   Parahippus   Pliohippus   Equus (domestic horse)

55 50 45 40 35 30 25 20 15 10 5 0
Time (millions of years from present)

chestnut

ergot

Through the study of fossils, paleontologists have found that my horse ancestors originated, lived and evolved in North America and eventually migrated around the globe. The planet looked much different then. Millions of years ago my horse ancestors were able to travel to Eurasia by crossing the Bering land bridge.

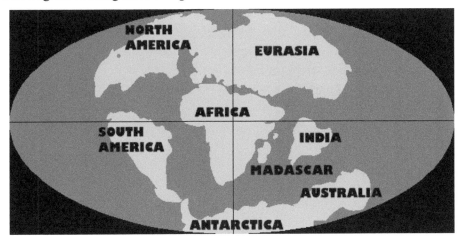

How the world looked millions of years ago

Can you see how the picture above looks different than the one below? Slowly the Earth began to change. In North America the mountain ranges began to uplift. In the center of the continents the climate became dryer. Lakes dried; their once-muddy bottoms eventually formed rock. The forests gave way to grassy plains. Seasons became more evident and ice began to form at the poles. The continents broke and drifted apart and the horses could not get back to the Americas. Eventually horses disappeared in the Americas. There were no horses at all in the Americas for thousands and thousands of years! So now you are wondering how I got here.

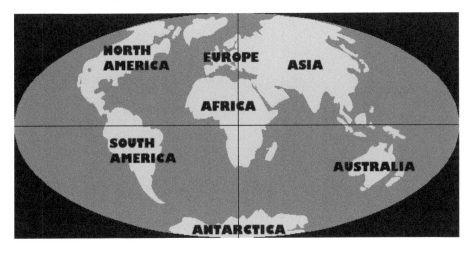

An archaeologist is a person who studies human history and prehistory by excavating sites and studying the artifacts and physical remains that they find.

Archaeologists have found more than one hundred caves in Europe with paintings of at least four thousand animals. Nearly one third of the animals in painted caves are paintings of my horse ancestors. Almost all of the caves are in southern France and northern Spain. One cave in France, called Chauvet Cave, has been dated to at least thirty-two thousand years ago. Other caves in Lascaux, France and Altamira, Spain are about fifteen thousand years old.

Painting of a horse from a cave in Lascaux France. Learn more about horse paintings here: https://www.worldhistory.org/Lascaux_Cave/

My early relatives ate leaves and fruit but as the world dried out, grasses became available and horse's teeth grew longer, with adaptations for breaking off and crushing the tougher grass. Wide grasslands were perfect for long, swift-legged herbivores and large herds of horses developed.

When humans first saw us, they hunted us and used us for food. Silly humans! It never occurred to them to domesticate us.

Your ancient human ancestors were nomads; they traveled in many directions, constantly in search of abundant food resources and new places to inhabit. But because they traveled on foot, they never traveled very far. They did not know about other civilizations. Imagine a world without a method to communicate other than transporting the message via human runners.

Since there is no written documentation to determine if horses were ridden or driven first, we can only imagine some daring person decided that getting on a horse or hooking a horse to something to pull might be a good idea – and not just to make a video that might go viral! They didn't have videos then any way.

Using horses for transportation changed the world much like computers and social media have changed the world today. Horses and riders, or horse-drawn carts, could now cover huge distances at great speed. As a result, trade routes developed and cultures began to intermingle. It's hard to imagine, in this age of cars and orbiting space stations, that a horse could be so important to human history – but they are and I can't wait to tell you all about my family.

Prehistoric cave drawings show us that early humans attempted to ride horses. Horse and rider cave painting in Dousche, Lorstan, Iran c 7000-8000 BC

Since early humans were nomads that meant that they moved to places where they could find food and water. One of the ways they moved was by following herds of horses. While the horse still remained a "wild animal", humans and horses grew closer together. Humans could attract the horse by providing food and providing shelter. Archaeologists found horse manure in the post holes of what might have been a stable built around 5000 BC in what is now Kazakhstan. Early humans found that they could milk the lactating mares and serve the milk to their own families. Some cultures today still use horses as a source for milk. Knife marks on thousands of ancient horse bones show that horses were raised for meat too.

Many cultures still use milk from horses. Learn more about the early domestication of horses in Kazakhstan here: https://www.world-archaeology.com/issues/issue-35/early-date-for-horse-domestication-in-kazakhstan/

The domestication of all animals was a process rather than an event and it occurred slowly over a period of thousands of years in different regions of the world. Cave paintings show us that early humans were very familiar with us; they hunted us, used us for milk and eventually did ride us. Most of these developments occurred before writing was invented so we depend on archaeological evidence to help us understand what happened. I am so glad that humans figured out how to partner with the horse because the domestication of my ancestors represents one of the most important turning points in human history. Archaeological evidence tells us that horses were domesticated about 5000 BC.

You are probably still wondering how I got here in America if all the horses left thousands of years ago. But, first I need to tell you about how breeding horses became very important in other parts of the world and how kingdoms and powerful rulers aspired to have large stables full of magnificent horses. Some of the oldest horse breeds in the world date back thousands of years. The horses of the Terra Cotta warriors found in China look very much like horses today don't they? And these were made over two thousand years ago! But it took a while before horses looked like this.

The Terracotta Army is a collection of terracotta sculptures depicting the armies of Qin Shi Huang, the first emperor of China. They were buried with the emperor in 210–209 BC with the purpose of protecting the emperor in his afterlife. Read more here about the Terra Cotta army here: https://en.wikipedia.org/wiki/Terracotta_Army

As horses spread out over Asia, Europe and Africa they evolved into the familiar shapes of present-day horses. Ancient horses adapted to living conditions wherever they lived. Horses that were born with favorable traits, were more likely to survive, reproduce and pass on beneficial traits to their offspring - this is called Natural Selection.

In the glacial landscapes, moors and heaths of the northern tundra both small, primitive ponies and the massive ancestors of the cold-blood breeds developed.

The forest type was less specialized. It survived into the eighteenth century and had considerable influence on the breeding of the warm-blood horse.

A very light long-legged horse with a striking ram-like head lived in the bleak mountainous regions of North Africa. It became the 'father' of the majestic horses of the Baroque era.

In the desert areas of south west Asia a type with fine limbs and built for speed evolved.

Although life in the steppe region did not demand any high degree of specialization, different breeds of steppe horse evolved. The gray small-headed, very lightly built steppe tarpan and the yellowish-brown heavier-headed Prjewalski's horse developed in the steppe region.

When horses were first domesticated, they were probably used as they were found in nature as a result of natural selection. But as the needs of humans changed, cultures bred horses for a variety of purposes: speed (for messaging or racing), size and power (for war), heft (for plowing and wagon pulling), smoothness of stride (for riding). During all of the wars and invasions, cultures and horses mingled. Eventually horse breeding changed from natural selection to selective breeding. That means that humans selected horses that suited their needs and bred them. So this is starting to make sense and explain how horses all look so different now. I don't look at all like the ancient horses and I don't look like a Thoroughbred race horse or a Clydesdale draft horse either and now we know the reason! Horses look the way they do in modern times because humans bred us to meet their purposes!

CHAPTER 4 ~ Horses Everywhere

Each culture in the ancient world was discovering things not knowing what other cultures were doing or discovering. One thing all peoples were doing almost everywhere was figuring out how to partner with my horse ancestors.

While the people in Egypt, Armenia, Babylon, Hatti and Matanni were using chariots to invade each other, the Chinese and other people were learning how to partner with the horse in many more ways.

When the chariot was invented, those who first used the new invention were able to storm their neighbors and seize valuable hunting and pasturing land rights. The chariot became the supreme military weapon. Chariots were light vehicles on two wheels, pulled by one or more horses. Usually there were two people in a chariot and they were both standing. One person was the driver and the other one was the fighter; he would have a bow and arrow or a javelin.

The oldest evidence of chariots to date comes from petroglyphs found in Armenia from 3000 BC. Petroglyphs are ancient rock carvings. The petroglyphs found in Armenia are the oldest pictures of men driving chariots.

Eventually, everywhere in Europe, the Middle East, India and China, kings, great pharaohs and even unimportant rulers used the chariot as their master weapon. Ancient art work created to honor the rulers shows them riding in chariots. They even included chariots and horses in their tombs as symbols of power.

Chariots were also used for hunting purposes and in sporting contests such as the Ancient Olympic Games and in the Roman Circus Maximus.

buried chariots from the Shang Dynasty 1660 BC - 1046 BC

Unlike technology today, that becomes out of date very rapidly, the use of the chariot declined very slowly starting around 500 BC. People still lived far apart and did not have a way to communicate and share information so some parts of Europe were just learning about chariots while other parts of the world had already been using chariots for hundreds of years!

Warfare was a large factor in early selective breeding. The horse came to be a valuable military asset - no longer just a food source of the nomads. Horse breeding became very important. Kingdoms and powerful rulers aspired to have large stables to supply their armies with horses for their chariots. Many different types and sizes of horses were used in war, depending on the form of warfare. The type of horse used depended on whether the horse was being ridden or driven and whether they were being used for cavalry charges, raiding, communication or supply.

Let's meet some of my ancestors from different places around the world.

The Steppes - The Horses of the Mongols - 3600 BC

Have you ever heard of the Steppes? Below is a map to show you where that is. Archaeologists have discovered new evidence of a horse-herding culture in the steppes more than five thousand years ago. People who lived there were nomads. Eventually they settled down and became farmers. They soon learned that the horse was a very important partner. They discovered that riding the horse allowed them to move much farther and to manage large herds more easily. They spread from Hungary to Mongolia. It did not take long before the entire population in the steppes was riding horses. In places other than the steppes, horses were very expensive to keep. Poor grazing land prevented the existence of large herds of horses. In other places in the world, only the nobility kept horses. This stalled chances of not only a cavalry to develop but also the general population riding or driving horses.

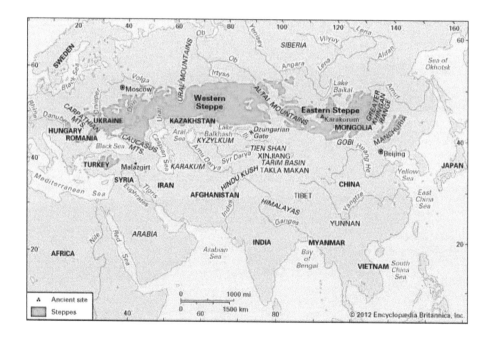

Mounted combat was innovated around 1000 BC by peoples of the western steppe. Did you know that the Great Wall of China was built because of horses? The Chinese warily watched these people in the steppes transform into mounted warriors who were expert bowmen. The Chinese knew this meant swift, repeated raids on the rich Chinese farmlands by mounted nomads. So, the Chinese decided to learn horsemanship and become archers. Successfully repelling the nomads for a time, the Chinese then began to build the Great Wall.

The Mounted warriors of the steppes were far superior to chariots in the battlefield. The Mongol Empire (1200 AD-1300 AD) represented the pinnacle of steppe power. At their peak, the Mongols controlled between eleven and twelve million square miles. In 1234 AD the Mongols, invaded China. By 1279 AD they were able to completely overthrow the Song Dynasty. Genghis Khan was the ruler of the Mongols at the time.

The horses of the Mongols still exist today! These are Mongolian horses in the picture below - they look much the same as they did in the time of Genghis Khan.

The Mongol army's battle tactics depended on their sturdy, agile and durable horses. A soldier could accurately shoot arrows with his bow from the back of his horse like in the picture above. The Mongol armies respected their horses and took good care of them. Every soldier had four to six horses. They would travel great distances; sometimes sixty to a one hundred miles a day, trading horses as they traveled. The fast, agile horses allowed them to have battle tactics that put them at a great advantage. The Mongol army trained every day in horsemanship, archery and hand-to-hand combat. They did not just ride horses that they found in the wild. They bred their horses. Archaeologists have found that the Mongol's horses were specifically bred for their lifestyle. The Mongolian horse is small like a pony, but it is not a pony breed. They have large heads, short necks, and wide bodies. They have strong, short legs with good joints and their hooves are sound and hard. Their stocky build makes them energetic, strong, and athletic. They have a high amount of stamina too. Horses that live in Mongolia today will spend time outdoors all year round. They are left to search for food on their own and they are used to surviving in temperatures ranging from -40°F to 86°F.

The Equids of the Sumerians 2600 - 2400 BC
(notice I did not say "horses" - find out why!)

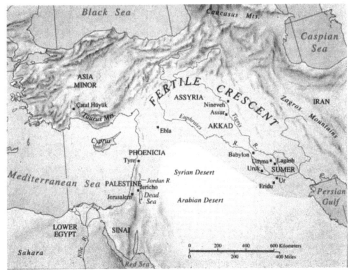

Sumer was first settled by humans from 4500 BC to 4000 BC. It was located in the Mesopotamia region of the Fertile Crescent situated between the Tigris and Euphrates rivers. Can you find Sumer on this map?

Somewhere around 2600 BC, there was a power struggle between the leaders of Kish, Erech and Ur, which lasted for the next four hundred years. During these wars Sumerians used heavy battlewagons with solid wheels drawn by wild asses called onagers. These battlewagons were very heavy because they did not have spoked wheels. They carried two men, a spear man and a driver. Both dismounted to fight. There are pictures of these battle wagons on a famous box called the Standard of Ur.

The Sumerians didn't invent wheeled vehicles, but they probably developed the first two-wheeled chariot in which a driver drove a team of animals. The onagers, instead of horses, were the animal of choice for the kings of Sumer. Boy were they silly to do that!

The first spoked-wheel chariot was used around 2000 BC. North-south trade routes brought both horses and spoked wheels to the Near East cultures of Mesopotamia, Iran, Syria, Persia and Egypt. Spoked wheels were a major improvement on the heavier solid wheels, allowing a lighter, speedier vehicle.

The Horses of the Ancient Greeks 1600 BC - 323 BC

It is rare to see chariots used in battle in ancient Greece because the mainland of Greece was so rocky. Chariots were used to transport warriors to and from battle, rather than for actual fighting. Horses were also used to bring the rider to the battlefield and then fighting was done on foot. This changed though when Greece engaged in war with armies from other parts of the world.

Horses were bred in northern Greece where there was more pastureland and it was less rocky. Thessaly was known for breeding amazing horses that had greater endurance, courage and beauty than horses from other parts of the world at the time. The horse they bred was called a Thessalian. They were strong horses. Their bodies were slim and their backs relatively straight, so the hindquarters were about level with the pronounced withers. Their legs had unusually short cannon bones. The horse had a good climbing ability which would be advantageous in the rocky terrain of Greece. Their heads had a straight profile with wide eyes and small ears.

Have you ever heard of Alexander the Great? This is a stature of him with his horse. Historians think his horse Bucephalus, was a Thessalian. The Thessalian breed had a rather coarse head.

Perhaps this is why Alexander's horse was called Bucephalus, (that means "ox head").

Have you ever heard of a Trojan Horse on your computer? Do you know where the name "trojan horse" comes from? The Trojan War was fought between Greeks and the defenders of the city of Troy sometime between 1750 BC and 1184 BC. Troy was famous for its horse breeding. The war lasted ten years until finally the Greeks decided to outwit Troy. Many Greek soldiers pretended to set sail for home, acting as if they had given up. In the midst of this pretend evacuation they made a large wooden horse and left it, as a supposed gift, at the gates of Troy. Troy loved horses so this seemed like an honorable gift! The Trojans pulled the mysterious gift into the city. When night fell, the horse opened up and a group of Greek warriors climbed out and opened the gates of the city to let the Greek army enter the city and conquer Troy. Nobody really knows how much of this story is true but now you know why a virus on your computer is called a "Trojan horse" since they look like something you should open but when you do, bad things happen to your computer.

The Horses of the Hyksos 1600 BC

You have probably seen lots of pictures of Egyptians with chariots but did you know that the horse is not native to ancient Egypt?

The Hyksos were people who settled in Egypt looking for grazing land for their cattle. The Hyksos were very difficult to expel from Egypt because they had wonderful horses and chariots, a method of warfare that the Egyptians had not seen before. But the horse soon became a much loved and prized possession for the Egyptian elite, particularly the Pharaoh. The horses first introduced to Egypt were smaller than those we are used to today. They were only 13.2 hands! A few horses though measured up to 15 hands. Most people in Egypt at the time used donkeys for agricultural work and horses were status symbols, used for such activities as hunting, warfare and ceremonial processions. They were almost always used to pull chariots rather than being ridden. However, battle scenes in the New Kingdom (1550 BC - 1069 BC) occasionally show individual soldiers mounted on them.

The Horses of the Mitanni and the Hittites 1400 BC - 1200 BC

Despite the fact that the Egyptians had a much larger army, the Hittites had more chariots and better horses. The Hittites were very powerful and attacked many of the regions surrounding their sprawling kingdom. The Hittites brought horses with them wherever they went and introduced the horse to many cultures. Their horses rank among the first horses in the Middle East. The Kingdom of Mitanni had alliances with mighty Egypt. They both needed to protect themselves from the threat of Hittites. The Egyptians did not breed horses at the time but rather, horses were imported, captured in war or received as tribute. By looking at ancient drawings, these horses appear to be small, elegant horses. The horses they had were the "desert type" that I told you about in chapter 3.

The first known written information about horses was in 1345 BC; a Mitannian horse-master known as Kikkuli wrote the *"Chariot Training Manual"*. It gave a detailed plan for training and caring for horses. The Kingdom of Mitanni spread from northern Mesopotamia down through Anatolia (which is modern-day Iraq through Turkey).

Nefertiti was queen alongside Pharaoh Akhenaten from 1353 to 1336 BC. In many paintings she is shown in positions of power and authority driving a chariot. In this picture, found on the wall of a tomb, she is driving her chariot, with a team of horses, whip in hand and without a driver. The famous horses of Nefertiti were probably Mittani. See how fine and elegant they look.

The Horses of the Kushites and Assyrians 800 BC - 600 BC

By the late eighth century BC the Assyrians had developed a deep appreciation of horses. They were able to conquer many countries and kingdoms because they were the first to organize their army into units with commanders. They also built large powerful chariots that could be pulled by four horses. The Assyrians obtained their horses by booty and trade. Records indicate that they received gifts of Egyptian horses the likes of which did not exist in their county. Nineveh was the capital of the Assyrian empire. The Nineveh Horse Reports were daily reports that detailed the numbers and types of horses received from other cites and provinces in the Assyrian empire. The records indicate thousands of horses over a three month period. References to Egyptian and Kushite horses in Assyrian texts indicate that the two North African countries actively bred horses and that the horses of Kush were a breed prized by Assyrian charioteers. Great armies need great and powerful horses. The breeding of horses is now happening in earnest. These horses were most probably home-bred under palace supervision.

As you can tell from these pictures, the Assyrian horses are shown to be massive with sturdy conformation, each animal having a muscular body and broad neck and of noble stature. All the animals exhibit a small-dished head notable for its alert expressiveness and rounded eyes.

Assyrian horses from Nineveh, 7th century BC.

Assyrian king Ashurbanipal on his horse thrusting a spear onto a lion's head. Alabaster bas-relief from Nineveh, dating back to 645-635 BC.

Marble slab from Ashurnasirpal II's palace. It is now in the British Museum. The image shows Ashurnasirpal II and his army advancing against a town. A battering ram is being drawn on a six-wheeled chariot

After the collapse of the Assyrian empire the finest and fittest horses bred in Assyrian-controlled territories spread to other parts of the Near East, to become the ancestors of later, equally fine breeds of horses.

The Horses of the Medes, Persians 1000 BC - 88 BC

The oldest tribes of Iran are: Persae (Persians) and Madai (Medes), which appeared in the ninth century BC in the Assyrian writings. Every spring, to begin their war season, the Assyrians either stole or demanded a tribute of horses from the Medes.

The Medes were the greatest horse-breeders of ancient times; they bred their horses in the vast fertile plains of Nisa - in what is now Southern Turkmenistan. Horses were an enormous part of Median life. They even played a large part in their religion. The Medes bred the Nisean horse, supposedly it is the finest horse the world has ever known. The breed is now extinct. The Nisean, was tall and swift and came in many colors; they were dark bay, white, chestnut and seal brown, but also were rarer colors such as black, roan, palomino and various spotted patterns. The Nisean was the mount of the nobility in ancient Persia. The ancient Greeks called the horse "Nisean" after the town Nisa where the horse was bred. The Chinese called the horse the Tien' Ma "the Heavenly Horse". The Nisean horse was the most valuable horse in the ancient world and they did not become extinct until the conquest of Constantinople in 1204 AD. Many Iberian type horses today are thought to be related to the Nisean.

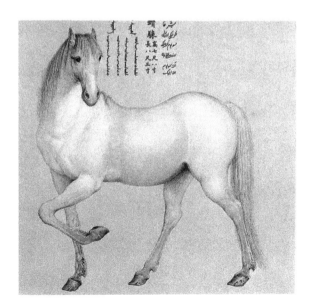

Nisean horse.

The Nisean horses were used for kings and generals to stand out on the battlefield and also demonstrate wealth and authority

Many breeds of horses were used by the Persians as their empire expanded. The Persians also had a finer horse known as the Armenian horse; now it is called the Caspian horse. It was very small; only about 12 hands. It was fast and agile with small ears and large nostrils.

Caspian horse

Persian cavalry

Only chariot horses' manes were kept long. Horses that were ridden had short manes and tied tails to prevent interference from the enemy and weapons. Only the forelock was kept long and, in battle, was tied with a bright ribbon. Persian cavalry soldiers used large, bright, heavily embroidered saddle cloths. The cloth was secured to the horse with breast and girth straps that were knotted around spacers because buckles were still not invented. Stirrups were not invented yet either.

Horses of the Scythians 800 BC - 300 BC

The Scythians' thought so highly of horses that their wealth was counted in horses. They left their mark in the history of warfare for their amazing equestrian skills. They were among the first to master mounted riding and to make use of composite bows while riding. Scythian men AND women mounted archers were admired and feared by Greeks, Romans, Persians and the Chinese, whose Great Wall was built to defend against them. Their military skill was recognized by the many civilizations around them and Scythian warriors frequently served as mercenaries in foreign armies, such as with the Persian empire.

The Scythians bred horses to suit their purposes. Their horses possessed speed and endurance and had many coat colors: including bay, black, chestnut, cream and spotted animals.

The Scythians believed that they needed horses in the after life so horses were buried with them when they died. Archaeologists found a dozen buried horses in full dress regalia in a Scythian burial site near the village in Kazakhstan. Their bits are made of wood and sculpted with animal figures, while their saddles are decorated with gold leaf, leather, and felt and rested on red saddle blankets. Each horse appears to have worn ornaments relating to an animal commonly represented in Scythian art. Ibex horns fashioned in wood were discovered near one horse and appear to have been worn on its head, while a griffin sculpture in the round with horns of leather was recovered near another pair of false horns. Wow! I kind of want headware like that!

Reconstructions of horses and tack trappings from Scythian royal burials, 5th century BC. From Renate Rolle, The World of the Scythians.

Horses in China 200 BC - 100 BC

Ancient China did not have enough good quality horses because the climate was not good and there was not enough hay. Dayuan, or Tayuan, was a kingdom in Central Asia in the Ferghana Valley from 250 BC to 125 BC. Can you find China and Dayuan on this map?

I told you about the Nisean horses that the Medes had. Well Dayuan possessed the most amazing horses known to the Chinese at the time. The Ferghana horse was also known as the "Heavenly Horse" in China or the Nisean horse in the West. Emperor Wu Di (reign 141 BC - 87 BC) wanted to trade bolts of silk for a thousand Ferghana horses and march them back to China. However, it was easier said than done. The horses were considered national treasures so the Dayuan refused to trade or even sell the horses. So began the first war ever fought over horses. It was called the "War of the Heavenly Horses". The people of Dayuan eventually offered the Chinese all the horses they wanted. The Chinese accepted the offer and went back home with three thousand horses. Ferghana horses were one of China's earliest major imports.

Ferghana Horse and Groom, Tang Dynasty

Horses of the Celts 1400 BC - 1100 AD

The Celts spanned across a wide geographic area and included numerous cultures and ethnicities. The Celts were fearsome fighters and renowned for their skill on horseback. Horses played an important role in Celtic culture. The Celts are the ones who sacked Rome in 390 BC. Thousands of fearless and yelling horsemen invaded a stunned Rome. This was the first time that the Romans encountered the Celtic cavalry. The horsemen of the Celtic cavalry had been riding since childhood. Eventually Rome became powerful again but most people who lived in Italy were afraid of invasions from Gaul. Gaul is the name given by the Romans to the territories where the Celtic Gauls lived. Gaul included present day France, Belgium, Luxemburg and parts of the Netherlands, Switzerland, Germany on the west bank of the Rhine, and the Po Valley in present Italy.

The first horses of the region probably arrived there on their own by walking there with or without the assistance of Stone Age man. From cave paintings it can be seen that some horses in the region were small, measuring at 11 hands, much like Shetland ponies. Some were fine boned similar to the horses used by the Hittites. There were also large boned 14 to 15 hand horses with convex heads.

Archaeological evidence shows a similarity of horses in the region at that time to the Exmoor Pony of today. The Exmoor Pony is small but hardy, with a height of only 11.1 to 12.3 hands. The breed's short legs, stocky build, and strong jaw suit the rugged terrain and coarse vegetation of its habitat. They have a dense undercoat to insulate them from freezing winter temperatures. There is also a long, oily, outer layer to protect them from chilling ice and snow. The fleshiness of their eyelids gives further protection from the cold. Additionally, the docks of their tails include long, coarse hairs known as a "snow chute"; these are designed to deflect water away from their groin and belly. The horses of Gaul were small compared to those of Italy. Caesar said that a pair of the Celtic horses pulling a chariot was so active and well trained that the horses could be turned in a narrow space or pulled up when going at full speed on a steep grade or even made to stand while the warrior ran out on the pole and stood on the yoke. From what Caesar described, the horses were under 12 hands. The Celtic ponies also often had a four beat lateral gait - a valuable asset for mounted horsemen without stirrups. Breeding of those that could do the four beat lateral gait was promoted. Today descendants of these smooth riding ponies still exist in Iberia (Garrano pony) and Iceland (Icelandic horse). I think horses are starting to look like me now!

Celtic chariot with horses

Garrano pony of today

Icelandic horse of today

Exmoor Ponies of today

Horses of the Romans 750 BC - 1453 AD

After the Celts sacked Rome, the Romans improved their military and became very powerful. Road systems often sprang up after Roman conquest of a region. The Roman road system was made up of about fifty thousand miles stretching from Syria in the east to Britain in the west. A person on horseback could cover three hundred sixty miles in two and a half days. Horse and mule carts averaged five to six miles per hour. This speed of transportation remained unequaled until the 19th century!

At the peak of the Roman Empire it included most of mainland Europe, Britain, much of western Asia, northern Africa and the Mediterranean islands.

The horse was an essential element in communications, transportation and fighting. The empire was vast and wherever the army went, the horses needed to be fed and watered too. The solution was aqueducts. Aqueducts are a complex network of ground works, pipes and other structures designed to transfer water from a source to a destination.

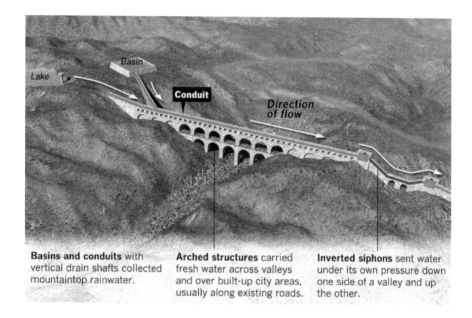

Basins and conduits with vertical drain shafts collected mountaintop rainwater.

Arched structures carried fresh water across valleys and over built-up city areas, usually along existing roads.

Inverted siphons sent water under its own pressure down one side of a valley and up the other.

Ancient Rome was a kind of society where class structure not only existed but was strictly enforced. The equestrian class was of economic importance and any man who could prove that he possessed a certain amount of wealth could be enrolled in the equestrian order. It was also possible for a member of the equestrian class to become a senator. A member of the equestrian order, known as an Eques, was required to serve up to ten years of service in the cavalry between the ages of seventeen and forty six. While farmers and merchants made do with local horses that were adapted to their needs and circumstances, the Eques were in agreement on where the best horses were raised and on the qualities of a good warhorse. The Roman army valued the horses bred by the Celtic tribes which formed the core of the cavalry units. Breeds favored for cavalry mounts also included those from Libya and Spain. Cavalry horses were fast, calm, rugged and obedient. Most Roman cavalry horses were around fourteen hands. The size and power of a horse were secondary considerations. The average horse would be on the small side compared to modern horses, but this was not considered a handicap in war; ancient cavalry tactics were built on maneuvering and raiding more than charging.

Statues could help to tell us about the "look" of ancient Roman horses. There were many statues of horses in ancient Rome. Ancient sources tell us that there were twenty-two "equi magni"—colossal bronze equestrian statues—that decorated the imperial capital.

This statue of Marcus Aurelius is the only one left standing today. The other equine statues were melted down during times of war or strife.

CHAPTER 6 ~ Horses in the Middle Ages

The horse defined the Middle Ages! Horses, along with mules and donkeys, were relied on for transportation, agriculture, war and recreation. A large part of the population was dedicated to occupations that used or cared for horses. In the Middle Ages roads were no more than dirt tracks that often turned into mud. Some goods were carried by pack horses and carts. Men traveled on horseback and ladies traveled in wagons covered in painted cloth. The wagons looked pretty, but they were very uncomfortable on bumpy roads since wagons of the Middle Ages had no springs. Travel in the Middle Ages was very slow; they could only travel thirty to forty miles a day.

In the Middle Ages the Christian church was growing due to the missionary work of monks. Monasteries often had stables for the horses of their guests. Many monasteries also kept their own horses so that they could travel and preach as needed. Horses were bred by Carthusian Monks beginning in the late Middle Ages. Some of the earliest written pedigrees in recorded European history were kept by the Carthusian monks. The horses bred by the monks were highly sought after by many people, including kings! Through the years the Carthusian monks guarded their bloodlines with passion, even denying an order to breed horses owned by royal stud farms into their stock. The PRE (Pura Raza Espanola) today can trace back to these horses. My stablemate Rosie is a PRE!!!

The Carthusian horse

My stablemate Rosie - he looks just like the horses the monks bred in the Middle Ages!!

During the Middle Ages horses were classified by their use, not by breed like we do today. The most valuable horse in the medieval stable was the horse of the knight, the **Destrier**. The Destrier was a very valuable horse so the knights even had rules to protect their horses in the tournaments. If you go to a museum and see some actual armor from the Middle Ages, you will be surprised that the horses were no bigger than most riding horses today; the Destriers were about 15 to occasionally 16 hands. That may seem small but that is still larger than most of the other horses of the Middle Ages. Most horses in the Middle Ages were the size of large ponies.

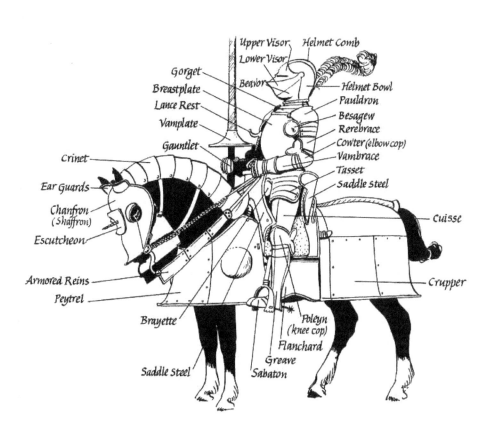

Coursers

Knights usually only used the Destrier for tournaments. Most knights also had other horses. **Coursers** were light, fast horses. They were the most common medieval warhorses. Coursers were sometimes preferred over Destriers in battle. The Courser was better for hard battle and fast pursuit because of their speed and stamina. Coursers were also used for hunting.

The **Rouncey** was the most affordable horse and usually the animal of choice for a poorer knight or squire. Rounceys were rather plain, general purpose horses who were also used for riding and as pack horses but never for pulling carts. They could also be trained for war. Rich knights supplied their attendants with Rounceys.

Rouncey

Palfreys

The ideal riding horse was the **Palfrey**. Palfreys could equal a Destrier in price, and for good reason; they had an extra gait known as the amble, which was fast, comfortable, and could be maintained by both rider and horse over long distances. This made traveling much easier and more pleasant. They were usually small horses, probably no taller than fifteen hands. The Palfrey was the horse of choice for noble ladies.

Sumpter

Food and goods in the Middle Ages were all transported by either pack horses or cart horses. The pack horse was faster than the cart horse, so it was used to transport perishable goods. The **Sumpter** was a grade horse used as a pack horse. Knights even used Sumpters to carry their armor when it was not being used. Most people think these horses were very small – pony size. There aren't that many illustrations of Sumpters but in England today there are still plenty of native ponies that were used extensively for hauling on the pack routes.

The **Hobelar** was a rugged and hardy pony which later became known as a "hobby" horse; they were also used as cart horses. The highest demand for cart horses was the transportation of hay and timber. Unlike pack horses, cart horses were used to move bulky or oddly shaped items. Cart horses were very important for moving goods around the cities. Most carts were light, two wheeled vehicles.

Hobelar

Affrus or Stott

At first, horses and oxen were commonly intermixed. The ox was stronger, cheaper to maintain and less temperamental but it lacked speed and endurance. The horse could work fifty percent faster and up to two hours longer a day since they didn't need to rest to digest food. Eventually innovations in harnessing and types of equipment made the use of the horse more practical. The horse used for farming was called an **Affrus** or **Stott.** They were usually smaller and cheaper than the cart or pack horse.

CHAPTER 7 ~ Horses in the Age of Discovery

The Renaissance (1350-1650) and the Age of Enlightenment (1650-1780) were part of the Age of Discovery. Things around the world were starting to change. Rather than loot and destroy, conquering armies were trying to mingle and learn new things from the people that they conquered. Beginning in the Renaissance, horses were bred for sporting endeavors as well as for war. Horses would be ridden for pleasure and used for transportation by carriage; so horses were bred specifically for those purposes. Improved farming methods called for a larger and stronger horse to be developed which led to the development of draft breeds. The world was coming out of the Dark Ages into a Renaissance and horses were going to continue to play an important role. The horse was even going to be an important part of the New World. We are getting closer to how I came to be - the horse is about to evolve into the horses we are familiar with today in modern times.

Horses of the Ottoman Empire

OU L'ART DE LA GUERRE. 353

SPAHIS.

Tom. III.

The Ottoman Army was the most feared army in Europe. The Ottoman Empire was one of the largest empires in history. It was in existence for six hundred years; the Ottoman Empire continued to exist until the first World War in 1914. The real strength of the army, and the fiercest warriors, were the horsemen known as the Sipahis. It was a state requirement for the Sipahis to breed horses. The rivalry between the Sipahis for the best horse provided for an increased quality of horses. The horses were bred for speed, strength, calmness and intelligence.

Horses of the Cossacks

The Cossacks were horsemen from the Russian Steppes who were descendants of the Mongol Golden Horde. They were free roaming outlaws who robbed and raided the countryside. In 1552 the Tsar Ivan asked the Cossacks to join his army to defeat the Tartars. At this point in history, people became interested in breeding horses in order to create horse breeds with specific abilities. From their many raids, the Cossacks began to gather horses from all parts of the area. The horses that were able to survive the lack of food and water in the harsh elements and endure the rigors of battle were used for breeding. It was indeed "survival of the fittest" that was important in their breeding program. The horse they produced was a medium-sized, rangy, agile and brave horse of astounding endurance and vitality. The horse became known as the Don horse and it still exits today.

The Beginning of Horse Breeding in England

Just when the English had finished the Hundred Years War, they started to fight among themselves. The War of the Roses was a civil war for the throne of England. The war lasted from 1455 to 1485 and in the end a new royal dynasty emerged - the Tudors. By the time of the Tudors, warfare in England was starting to change. New weapons of war, early cannon, war ships and heavy-duty castles and forts meant the use of horses in open battle was decreasing. Horses started being used more for sport and status.

England lost many horses during the War of the Roses so, Henry VIII passed several laws in relation to horse breeding and started to import thousands of horses from abroad. Remember in the Middle Ages that horses were only of a "type". Now horses were starting to be bred for specific qualities and traits. Henry VIII was interested in improving both type and size of British horses. Laws passed in 1535 and 1541 required that all mares should reach 13 hands high and stallions 14 hands. Henry had royal stables for breeding horses used for hunting and racing. He set up stables at Greenwich where his horses were trained and their stamina and speed improved.

King Henry VIII followed by Sir Anthony Brown, Master of the Horse. From the Cowdray Engravings portraying the King's visit to Portsmouth, July 19, 1545.

France and the Breeding and Training of Horses

Louis XIV was king from 1638 to1715. He is best known for the magnificent palace that he built at Versailles. He loved horses and built extravagant stables at Versailles. The Versailles stables could house over seven hundred horses and had over thirty carriage buildings. At the end of his reign he had one thousand seven hundred horses. In political terms, a King's horsemanship skills were a symbol of his ability to govern well. One of the most famous Grand Écuyers (master of the horse for the king) was Antoine De Pluvinel (1552 -1620). He wrote a book entitled, "L'Instruction du Roy en l'exercice de monter à cheval"(instructing the King in the art of horse-riding.) Many people still read his book today. He is best known for his kind training methods. Much of dressage today is based on his ideas and methods.

The new methods showed kindness to the horses. Almost all of the horses in the stables at Versailles came from England, Ireland, Spain, North Africa and northern Europe. The horses were considered to be the most elite collection of horses any place in the world at the time. There was now a national pride in breeding horses specific to the needs of the country and often, the wishes of the nobility. One of the most famous French breeds that was perfected during this time period was the Percheron.

stables at Versailles   *Percheron horse*

The Hapsburgs and Horses

During the Renaissance, Vienna, Austria, was a leader in science and fine arts. Austria was ruled by the House of Hapsburg from 1273 to 1918. During the Renaissance Charles V, of the House of Hapsburg, was the most powerful monarch in Europe.

Charles' health began to fail so he abdicated. After the abdication of Charles V in 1556, the Hapsburg dynasty split into the branch of the Austrian (or German) Hapsburgs, led by Ferdinand, Charles' brother, and the branch of the Spanish Hapsburgs, initially led by Charles' son Philip.

There was a need for light, fast horses for use in the military and for the classical riding that was being taught to nobles. In 1562, Maximilian, Ferdinand's son, founded a Spanish horse stud farm in Kladruby, Bohemia (now the Czech Republic). Maximilian's brother, Charles II, Archduke of Inner Austria decided to also establish a new stud farm and the Spanish horse was considered the ideal horse breed. Since the soil and climate in the Karst region is similar to that of Spain, Lipica was chosen as the perfect spot for the new farm. The Lipica stud farm was established in 1580 and the first horses were bought from Spain in 1581. Both breeding programs still exist today.

Riding horses and light carriage horses came from the Lipizza stud farm. The famous Spanish Riding School in Vienna, Austria was first named during the Hapsburg Monarchy in 1572. Records show that a wooden riding arena was first commissioned in 1565, but it wasn't until 1729 that Emperor Charles VI commissioned the white riding hall that is used today. The Spanish Riding School was named for the Spanish horses that were the base of the Lipizzan breed.

Lipizzaners at the Spanish Riding School

The Kladrub stud produced heavy carriage horses used to pull the imperial coach, usually in a four or six-in-hand, at ceremonies and funerals.

Kladrubers in harness at the National Stud at Kladruby

The Influence of Spanish Horses

So what kind of horses are these amazing Spanish horses that were bred by the Hapsburgs and still bred today?

On September 28, 1527 King Philip II of Spain published a decree that a new horse breed should be created. He wanted to breed a distinctly magnificent horse. Philip II founded the State breeding real Yezuada de Castilla (Royal Horse herd). Spain was at the height of its power at this time. The conquistadors conquered South and Central America with the Spanish horse and riding schools throughout Europe were filled with Spanish horses for hundreds of years. The Spanish horse became the world's most popular riding horse. Remember the PRE (Pura Raza Espanola - Pure Spanish Horse) that I told you about that the monks were breeding in the Middle Ages? Well this is the horse that the Spanish were breeding that was in such demand; this horse left its footprint all around the entire world and they are still bred in Spain today. The nobility at the time all rode Spanish horses.

Queen Isabella
1451 -1504
Queen of Spain

King Charles I
1600-1649
King of Great Britain.

Louis XIV
1638-1715
King of France

Five hundred years ago there were thousands of bison, deer and dogs in North America and there were llamas in South America but, there were no horses. Remember, they all left thousands of years ago. These animals had to come back from Europe with the early explorers, early settlers and colonists.

Spanish horse in sling during crossing. Many ships that transported horses had slings to keep horses upright

Christopher Columbus was well received in the court of King Ferdinand and Queen Isabella after his first voyage in 1492. The first horses known to arrive in the New World were transported by Christopher Columbus on his second voyage in 1493. By 1494 Columbus was so convinced of the value of horses for military and civilian use that he wrote to the Spanish sovereigns requesting that horses be included on all future voyages.

Over the next decades, the Spanish, French, Dutch and British all competed for control of the New World - and they all brought horses with them when they came to the New World.

Today, there are many breeds of horses in the Americas that are the result of cross breeding of the horses brought by the early settlers and explorers.

Early settlers to the Americas probably assumed the needs for horses would be the same as they had been in Europe – transportation, warfare and farming. Little did they know that just surviving would be so difficult. Breeding horses for a purpose did not begin until the Americas were well established. Until the last years of the 18th century, livestock received a low amount of care. Domestic animals could survive only if they were strong enough to last through the winter, relying mainly on forests and natural meadowland for subsistence.

The first concern for the early settlers was size. In the early Americas many of the horses brought from Europe were small. Settlers soon learned that a larger, more powerful and more versatile horse was needed. The Dutch horses were over 14 hands and the English horses were under 13 hands; most likely Irish Hobby horses. Stringent regulations were adopted against allowing under sized colts and stallions to wander as they pleased. To foster quality in American horses, as early as 1668, the court of Massachusetts decreed that only horses "of comely proportions and 14 hands in stature" could graze on town commons. A law was enacted by William Penn in Pennsylvania in 1687 which set a minimum height of 13 hands for free ranging horses. Any horse more than eighteen months old and less than 13 hands had to be gelded. This really did not accomplish what was hoped. It was not until the close of the colonial days when farmers had facilities for breeding stock that there was an increase in the size of the horses. In the decree below a "stone" horse is a stallion,

Whereas the Breed of Horses in the Country is utterly spoiled, whereby that useful Creature will become a burthen, which otherwise might be benificial, and the occasion thereof is conceived to be through the smalness and badness of Stone Horses and Colts that run in Commons and Woods;

O   If

Order for the best improvement of Stone Horses

For prevention whereof, This Court doth Order and Enact, and be it Ordered and Enacted by the Authority hereof, That no Stone Horse above two years old shall be suffered to go in Commons and Woods at liberty, unless he be of comely proportion and sufficient stature, not less then *fourteen Hands high,* reckoning *four Inches to a Handful,* and such a Horse to be viewed and allowed by the major part of the Select men of the Town where the owner lives.

And if any person or persons turn any Stone Horse upon the Commons, or at liberty, or in the Woods, being not viewed and allowed as before, he or they shall forfeit *twenty shillings* a Month for every Stone Horse running at liberty, after he is a *two years old;* which penalty is to be taken by Warrant of the Select Men, and imployed to the Towns use, and if the Select Men of any Town do neglect their duty in taking their fines, and viewing such as are brought in, according to this Law, they shall forfeit *twenty shillings* to the County Treasury; and this Law to be in force the first of *October* next. [*1668.*]

Although there are many breeds of horses in the Americas today, the breeds and types listed next are those that developed in early America.

Narragansett pacer: etching from Frank Forester's Horse and Horsemanship of the United States and British Provinces of North America 1857

Travel was difficult in early America due to the long distances between towns and the lack of roads so a pacing/ambling horse was the answer. The pacing horses of Rhode Island were sought after for travel by many. The **Narragansett Pacer** made valuable contributions to many horse breeds of North America. The horse is named for the area from which they developed – the Narragansett Bay area of Rhode Island. Their ancestors were probably among the English and Dutch horses which arrived in Massachusetts between 1629 and 1635. The Narragansett Pacer was known as a saddle horse that provided a comfortable ambling gait that was sure-footed; they had great endurance. The Narragansett Pacer was the primary export and chief source of income for the area. It was bred in vast numbers in the 1700s and exported to Cuba, Barbados and West India Islands to be used on the plantations. This continued into the 18th century. The breed reigned as the most desirable saddle horse for a century and a half. The breed eventually became extinct as colonial roads improved and people began to drive trotting horses more than ride these ambling, smooth gaited horses. The sturdy qualities of the Narragansett pacers have been perpetuated also by James Fenimore Cooper in his tales of the American wilderness. He seats his heroine, Alice Munro, on a Narragansett Pacer in "The Last of the Mohicans". The horses were evidently still obtainable in Cooper's day and he must have been an admirer of the breed, for he brings them into his stories frequently. George Washington owned a pair of Narragansett Pacers, which he highly valued. He wrote about racing them in his diary. Esther Forbes, Paul Revere's Pulitzer Prize winning biographer, argues forcibly that the horse that Revere rode from Charlestown to Lexington was a Narragansett Pacer but this has been debated.

Read more about the Narragansett horses here: http://www.newenglandhistoricalsociety.com/narragansett-pacer-lost-horse-new-england-colonies/ and https://archive.org/stream/ horseraisinginco00phil/horseraisinginco00phil_djvu.txt)

The **Conestoga Horse** was developed in the United States during the 18th and early 19th centuries for pulling the famous Conestoga wagons that were produced in Lancaster County, Pennsylvania. The Conestoga Valley was settled in the early 18th century. It was then wilderness but a country of unsurpassed fertility. Its first homemakers were farmers. They came from the upper Rhine country and Switzerland. With them came a good number of French Huguenots. These people needed horses for many things, all of which were hard work. These horses were not bred by any scientific system but by a process of natural selection. As generation succeeded generation a horse evolved that met the demands placed upon it by understanding owners. As settlers began heading west from Pennsylvania, more and more horses were needed to pull their heavy wagons. The Conestoga wagon was designed to meet this need, and the Conestoga horse was called upon to power it. In hauling these wagons over the Allegheny Mountains the Conestoga won its place in the story of American transportation. It is thought that horses owned by George Washington may have been used for breeding in the development of Conestoga horses. *(Read more about Conestoga horses here: http://articles.mcall.com/1988-03-06/ entertainment/2614046_1_five-horsesconestoga-breed)*

CONESTOGA.
Owned by John Eshelman, of Martie, Pa.

Conestoga Horse, engraving from the Report of the Commissioner of Agriculture for the year 1863

Conestoga Wagon 1883

FINALLY!!!!!!! We are getting closer to the **Making of Me!!!!!**

Statue of Justin Morgan in Vermont at the University of Vermont Morgan Horse farm Dedicated in 1921 at UVM.

The **Morgan Horse** is one of the earliest horse breeds developed in the United States tracing back to the foundation sire, Figure, born in 1789. The horse was later named Justin Morgan after his owner. Morgans served many roles in early American history, being used as farm horses, driving horses, for harness racing, as well as general riding animals and as cavalry horses during the American Civil War on both sides of the conflict. Morgans have influenced other major American breeds, including the American Saddlebred, American Quarter Horse, Tennessee Walking Horse and the Standardbred. Justin Morgan also proved to be one of the greatest breeding horses of all time. As the saga of the little stallion grew, countless mares were bred to him. So prepotent were the genes of this stallion that no matter what type of mare he was bred to, be the mare of heavy draft or refined racing-type, his offspring inherited his image and abilities. While most breeds develop by breeding horses of similar characteristics to each other, Justin Morgan's ability to pass his characteristics to his offspring for generations to come allowed this single stallion to found an entire breed in his likeness. Today, every registered Morgan traces back to Justin Morgan through his best-known sons Bulrush, Sherman and Woodbury. (*Read more about Morgans horses here: https://en.wikipedia.org/wiki/Morgan_horse and http://afs.okstate.edu/breeds/horses/morgan/index.html*)

By the time the Morgan horse started to become popular, citizens in the country had already fought a revolution to become independent and the new country was beginning to grow.

On February 4, 1789, electors chose George Washington to be the first president of the United States - the same year that Figure was born. I am going to introduce you to all of the stallions in my sire line all the way back to Figure.

The Morgan breed grew with the country and it's a wonderful story of **How I Came to Be!**

This is what registration certificates look like for a Morgan horse. This is my registration certificate; it shows all of the sires and dams for four generations. The Morgan horse registry has information tracing the breeding of horses back to Justin Morgan; that's why I can trace my family back to 1789. On the next two pages are pictures of horses in my sire line with their names and year of their birth - all the way back to Figure/Justin Morgan.

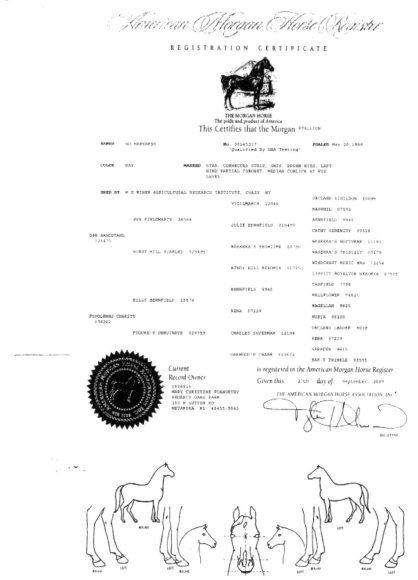

HD Harkness 1998

DPR Bandstand 1991

HVK Filedmarch 1975

Vigilmarch 1957

Orcland Vigildon 1947

Ulendon 1933

Ulysses 1927

Bennington 1908

General Gates 1894   Denning Allen 1874   Honest Allen 1855

Ethan Allen 1849   Black Hawk 1833   Sherman Morgan 1808

Figure (Justin Morgan) 1789

I'm going to tell you how I came to be by starting in 1789 with Figure - Justin Morgan's horse.

Justin Morgan 1747-1798

Justin Morgan was a descendant of Miles Morgan, an early pioneer of Springfield, Massachusetts and ancestor of financier J.P. Morgan. Springfield, a cavalry depot during the American Revolution, was a hive of horse activity. While starting his family, Justin Morgan rented horses for stud, ran a farm and served as a part-time tax collector. Then, after the war, people couldn't pay their taxes because of hard times and lack of currency. The state could seize tax collectors' property if they didn't come up with enough tax receipts. Morgan couldn't, and he got hauled into court. Around 1788, he moved his family to the independent Republic of Vermont, perhaps to escape Massachusetts taxes. In Randolph, Justin Morgan farmed, sold liquor, bred horses, served as town clerk and wrote music. He also taught penmanship and singing. He traveled widely, as far as the Pennsylvania, New York and Maryland.

Sometime around 1792 Justin Morgan received a colt in payment of a debt. He went to Springfield, Massachusetts to get the horse and walked him back to Randolph, Vermont. The horse was only 14 hands tall and weighed about 950 pounds. Mr. Morgan was a musician so he named the horse "Figure". He must have thought, "I needed the payment of a debt, not a horse that will cost me money to care for!" So he put the horse to work in order to earn his keep. Any task that required power - like pulling logs and heavy skids - the horse did with ease. Morgan even leased Figure to clear land for $15 a year. Catch races were popular in early America and Figure proved that he was very hard to beat - even after a long day of hard work! In 1796, Figure easily won a race against two New York horses in Brookfield, Vermont. The stretch of road he raced is known today as the "Morgan Mile".

Depiction from the 1800s of Figure, born 1789 the Justin Morgan Horse

Morgan recognized that his horse was indeed a genetic mutation and stood him at stud. Figure had an exceptional temperament and willingness to work. Above all he was sturdy, resistant to illness, required little feed and upkeep, was curious and trusting. Soon everyone wanted to breed their mares to "Justin Morgan's horse". Morgan owned Figure for about three years, advertising him for stud in Randolph and Lebanon, New Hampshire, and Royalton, Williston and Hinesburg, He eventually traded the horse for land in Moretown, Vermont.

Figure had eleven more owners during his life. Three of Figure's children then became foundation bloodstock: Woodbury, Bulrush and Sherman. By the 1830s, Vermont farmers were selling Morgan horses outside the state and many paid off their mortgages with the proceeds. *(some information courtesy of New England Historical Society)*

No matter what type of mare he was bred to, he passed on all of his characteristics. The most amazing thing about Justin Morgan is that prepotency even two hundred plus years later! Prepotency is the ability of one parent to impress its hereditary characteristics on its progeny (offspring). One of the best known examples in the horse world of prepotency is Justin Morgan, the sole founding sire of the Morgan horse breed. His ability to repeatedly and reliably stamp his offspring with his own desirable characteristics is the reason given for the breed's existence. Isn't that an incredible story of how a breed of horses was started?!

I'm excited to tell you about all of the amazing horses in my sire line starting with Figure's son, Sherman.

Sherman Morgan. (Courtesy Morgan Horse Magazine)

Sherman born 1808

I come from the Sherman line of Morgans. Sherman was bred by James Sherman, a native of Rhode Island and veteran of the Revolutionary War. James Sherman eventually moved his family to Vermont, purchasing a farm two miles west of Lyndon Center at a location known as Cold Hill.

The dam of Sherman Morgan was one of the last of the Narragansett Pacers, which had been very popular in of Rhode Island for a hundred years. She was used there for several years where she had a reputation as an excellent saddle horse. She was purchased by James Sherman and taken with him when he moved to Vermont with the express intent to breed her to the Justin Morgan horse. Described as a chestnut mare with three white feet and stripe in face, she was of elegant form with a fine head and small expressive ears, long neck which she carried well up and was a spirited traveler with a kind and pleasant disposition. The Shermans referred to her as being "of Spanish blood".

Born in 1808, Sherman Morgan was a bright chestnut and at maturity he was 14.1 hands, weighing 925 lbs. His head was lean and well shaped, ears small and fine, eyes inclined to be small, but full, prominent and lively; his legs were broad, flat and sinewy. He had a capital chest, with the breast bone very prominent; the shoulders were large and well placed, the neck excellent, the mane and tail full. His hips were long and deep, the loins broad and muscular. Most of the year he was kept constantly at hard work upon the Cold Hill farm and, in the winter, he ran in a two-horse team with another son of Justin Morgan, from Lyndon, Vermont to Portland, Maine, a route of more than one hundred forty miles. The little team became famous at every inn along the route as they were often matched against horses of any size whenever the opportunity arose, but none could beat them. Sometime before 1819, Sherman was sold, changing owners several times, and eventually coming into the hands of John Bellows in 1829. He was there and remained with Bellows until his death in 1835, having attained the reputation of being the best sire in New England during his time.

Black Hawk was the most famous grandson of Justin Morgan. He was jet black in color, 15.1 hands and weighing about 1,000 pounds. He was bred by Benjamin Kelly and foaled in April 1833, the property of Ezekiel Twombly, both of Durham, New Hampshire. Sired by Sherman Morgan, son of Justin Morgan, his dam was a handsome black Thoroughbred mare. She stood 16 hands, and weighed about 1,100 pounds.

Black Hawk born 1833

Black Hawk was described as follows: "He comes nearer to our beau ideal of a perfect driving horse than any other animal we have ever seen. (That sounds like me!!!) Possessed of abundance of spirit and life, there is also manifest a quietness and evenness of temper that make him under all circumstances perfectly controllable; his step is nervous and elastic, but no unnecessary steps are taken. His style of movement is bold and fearless, while every motion is instinct with grace." Black Hawk was said to be more like Justin Morgan than any of his sons. During the last twelve years of his life alone he was bred to one thousand seven hundred seventy two mares!

America was growing and horses were very much a part of that growth! The revolution that created the country had ended only forty-seven years before. The Erie Canal - the pathway that would open up the West - had been completed and here was plenty of land available to start a new life. Construction of the National Road began in 1811 and followed the path of old buffalo and Indian trails through the Allegheny Mountains to the plains of the Mid West. At its completion in 1839 it stretched all the way to Vandalia, Illinois. It was a bustling conduit to the West for pioneers and traders. In the 1840s several breeders in Vermont and western New Hampshire began efforts to concentrate the Morgan lines. By locating second, third, and fourth generation descendants of the original Morgan horse, they established the foundations of the breed. By the mid-1850s, Morgans were selling for high prices and were widely distributed across the United States.

As emigrants trekked westward in the 19th century, the frontier advanced with them. Vermonters initially emigrated to northern New York, then to Ohio. By the 1850's, Morgans could be found in Michigan, Illinois and Wisconsin in large numbers. In the U.S. Census of 1850, Vermont had the highest number of its native-born population living outside their native state of Vermont (41%).

To provide transport for their wagons and goods, Vermonters took their Morgan horses with them. Ohio agricultural journals mention Morgan horses frequently in the 1850's. Two Morgan stallions, Black Hawk and Hale's Green Mountain 42, were shown at Midwestern state fairs in the early 1850's. Both attracted much attention and were widely admired.

In what was then the west (but is now the Midwest), Morgans were used to pull stagecoaches, for light farm work and as all around family buggy horses. The high demand for them created high prices. Some Vermonters became concerned about the possible depletion of their breeding stock. One writer warned Vermont farmers not to be tempted to sell all their best stock as they needed to retain some to be able to continue to supply the market. The high prices were difficult for many Vermonters to resist though.

In the 1850's Morgans could be found throughout Ohio and Michigan and as far west as Wisconsin. They were so popular that many less-than-honest folks were claiming Morgan ancestors for horses that had no Morgan blood in their ancestry. Complaints appeared in the press about the problem to no avail. As the Western Frontier continued to expand, the Morgan horse influence continued to spread also. As ranches were established, they proved to be reliable and enduring mounts. Richard Sellman of Texas established his ranch at this time with a relative of mine, Red Oak by General Gates (I'll tell you all about him in a little bit). By the early 20th century he had the largest herd of Morgans in America. He registered over 300 mares and a few stallions, but most of the colts were simply gelded and used as ranch horses. During the Gold Rush days of 1848 a herd of 125 Morgans was taken west to California. Most survived the trip and were sold for high prices upon arrival. Other Morgans arrived in California as well with the stallions often commanding high stud fees. St. Clair sired over 600 offspring while standing at stud in Sacramento in the mid-19th century. *(Read more about Morgans in early America here: http://morganhorseguide. com/tag/famous-morgan-horses/)*

Ethan Allen born 1849

Morgans set world trotting records when the sport of harness racing was in its infancy. Black Hawk and his son Ethan Allen were nationally famous and became household names. The majority of Morgans, however, just did their daily work willingly and efficiently. They were highly regarded as general-purpose horses capable of performing a wide variety of tasks. The most famous of Black Hawk's sons was Ethan Allen, who started in fifty nine races and won first prize money in forty four. Named Champion Trotting Stallion of the World when only four years old, his record was 2:25 ½ in single harness, and 2:15 "to pole." This peculiar means of racing involved hitching a great strong Thoroughbred running horse in the traces beside the trotter and adjusting the breeching so the runner would take the full weight of the wagon. This was supposed to provide an advantage in allowing the trotter to go his best gait while unencumbered by weight. However, this was largely offset by the distraction of having the much larger Thoroughbred going alongside on a dead run. The trotter meanwhile was supposed to stay focused and keep his perfect trotting gait without breaking. Few horses could do it, but Ethan was one who was actually good at it. His well known record of 2:15 with running mate was made in the match race against Dexter when he was eighteen years old.

The trotting horse weather vane that you see on lots of houses and barns is an image of my ancestor Ethan Allen!

Dexter, Ethan Allen and mate: In their wonderful race, over the fashion course, June 21st 1867. Match for $2,000 mile heats best 3 in 5

Morgans were becoming well known for their temperament and athletic ability. As the popularity of Morgans grew so did the young country but the growth was not without problems. Soon the country was involved in a Civil War and Morgans played an important part. Morgan horses are known to have been used in both the Union and Confederate armies. Due to the quality of the Morgan horses and their physical attributes, they were in high demand. They were hardy and their thick winter coats enabled them to survive without shelter during bad weather, they were able to survive on scant forage, their resilient skin reduced saddle sores, and the Morgans were highly trainable and willing to please. The following regiments of the cavalry were mounted on Morgans when they were first organized.

- First Maine Cavalry
- First Vermont Cavalry
- Second Michigan Cavalry
- Third Michigan Cavalry
- Fourteenth Pennsylvania Cavalry
- Fifth New York Cavalry Company H
- First Rhode Island Cavalry (Morgans and French Canadian horses)

I want to tell you about some of the brave and amazing Morgans that served in the Civil War. Some are my close relatives!

Pink was the favorite mount of Colonel John Hammond of the Fifth New York Cavalry of Crown Point, New York. This unit mustered into the war in October, 1861. At the time the unit purchased 108 Morgan horses. They were a favorite breed for their sturdiness and perseverance. Only 8 horses survived the war. One was Pink. He had accompanied Col. Hammond in 88 skirmishes and 34 battles. After the war Pink returned to Crown Point with Col. Hammond. He died at the age of 30 years in 1886. Colonel Hammond had a monument erected to honor Pink in a small park in Crown Point, New York. The monument reads:

"This horse carried his master 25 years. Was never known to show fatigue while other horses in cavalry and flying artillery were dying from want of food and exhaustion. He was present in 88 skirmishes and 34 battles, notably Winchester, Orange Court House, Second Bull Run, Hanover, Pa., Gettysburg, Hanover, Va., Brandy Plains, Buckland Mills, the Wilderness, Spottsylvania Court House, North Anna, Ashland, White Oaks Swamp, Reams Station."

Rienzi

At the start of the Civil War the Second and Third Michigan Cavalry were mounted on Morgan horses. Union General Philip Sheridan's famous mount Rienzi was presented to him by Captain Archie Campbell of the Second Michigan Cavalry. Rienzi is a close relative to me! He was the favored mount of Sheridan; a black gelding of Black Hawk lineage; Rienzi was ridden in battle by Sheridan during the rest of the war. His name was changed to "Winchester" by Sheridan after he carried Sheridan on his famous ride from Winchester, Virginia, to Cedar Creek, Virginia on October 19, 1864, in time to rally his troops and turn almost certain defeat into victory. While Cedar Creek was his most famous engagement, Winchester and Sheridan were actually together for more than forty others. The horse was wounded in battle several times and lived to be almost 20 years old. Winchester was present at Appomattox Courthouse in April 1865 for the official surrender of the Confederate Army. I am related to Rienzi through the Black Hawk line of Morgans. I think some General would have been proud to have me for their mount too!

Stonewall Jackson's most widely-known horse, Little Sorrel, was a Connecticut-bred Morgan. It fell into Confederate hands when Rebels captured a train near Harper's Ferry hauling horses acquired by the Federal government for army usage. Originally intending to give the horse to his wife, Jackson paid the quartermaster $150 for the gelding, naming him "Fancy." But after riding the horse, Jackson found the animal's gait so pleasing he remarked, "A seat on him was like being rocked in a cradle." Deciding to keep the horse for himself, it quickly became known as "Little Sorrel" once Jackson began using it as his regular mount. Although not looking the part of the classic "war-horse," Little Sorrel had the reputation of remaining calm in battle while also possessing remarkable stamina on long marches. Records show that not only did the gelding charge into untold numbers of battle, he often covered over forty miles in a day. Troops said they never, ever saw fatigue in that horse. Not only was he brave, but he was full of personality Troopers reported that Little Sorrel would lay down on the picket line and receive apples fed to him by the men. After surviving the war, the gelding was described as a rascal with a mouth that could undo latches, let down bars and liberate every horse in the barn. And like his earlier master, he would lead his command into new fields of opportunity, removing fence rails whenever he wanted. Jackson was riding Little Sorrel when wounded on May 2, 1863 at the battle of Chancellorsville. The horse remained on the battlefield after Jackson was removed to receive medical attention and was later found by two artillery soldiers, neither of whom recognized it as Jackson's horse. One of the soldiers rode the horse for several days until it was discovered to be Little Sorrel, at which point the horse was turned over to General J.E.B Stuart. He in turn gave the animal to Anna Jackson, who took Little Sorrel with her to North Carolina to live at her father's farm. In 1883, Anna donated Little Sorrel to the Virginia Military Institute (VMI), where the animal was permitted to leisurely graze the parade grounds for the next two years. The horse was then relocated to the Confederate Soldiers' Home in Richmond, Virginia, where he subsequently died at the age of 36 in 1886.

General Joshua Lawrence Chamberlain was a writer; he penned many articles and reminiscence after the war - many about his horse Charlemagne. During the autumn of 1863 (after Gettysburg), a small Morgan horse with scars and sores from pack-service was captured from the Confederates. Chamberlain took a liking to the horse and bought him for $150 from the U.S. Government. With attention, grooming, and TLC, Charlemagne's appearance improved drastically and he became an affectionate animal-friend. Horse and rider were wounded many times. Joshua Chamberlain, mounted on Charlemagne, was the first person to receive the white flag from the Confederates at Appomattox Court House on April 12, 1865. Chamberlain also received the surrender of the arms of Lee's Army of Northern Virginia while mounted on Charlemagne. In Chamberlain's own words: "Instructions had been given; and when the head of each division column comes opposite our group, our bugle sounds the signal and instantly our whole line from right to left, regiment by regiment in succession, gives the soldier's salutation, from the "order arms" to the old "carry"— the marching salute. Gordon at the head of the column, riding with heavy spirit and downcast face, catches the sound of shifting arms, looks up, and, taking the meaning, wheels superbly…with profound salutation as he drops the point of his sword to the boot toe; then facing to his own command, gives word for his successive brigades to pass us with the same position of the manual, honor answering honor."

Surrender of the Army of Northern Virginia to the Army of the Potomac Confederate (on right) coming forward to surrender arms to the Union troops (on left) at "Appomattox Court House. Title inscribed above image. - Inscribed next to title: as described to me by Genl. Chamberlain, who recd the surrender. Sketch by John R. Chapin for Harper's magazine

In the 1988 "The Last Salute" by Don Troiani General Joshua L. Chamberlain's Union soldiers stand at attention as Confederate General John Brown Gordon touches his sword to his boot top in a gesture of honor during the formal surrender at Appomattox Court House, Virginia

Together they paraded in the Grand Review of the Armies in June 1865. Charlemagne caused some mischief for his general during the Grand Review of the Army of the Potomac when a young lady tried to give Chamberlain a wreath of flowers. In Chamberlain's own words, "…my excited horse, [was] stirred by the vastness, the tumult, the splendor of the scene. He had been thrice shot down under me; he had seen the great surrender. But this unaccustomed vision, – he had never seen a woman coming so near before, – moved him strangely, Was this the soft death angel – did he think? calling us again, as in other days? For as often as she lifted the garland to the level of my hand, he sprang clear from earth…. From that time my horse was shy of girls, – sharp eyes out for soft eyes, – I dare say, for his master's peace and safety!" Charlemagne returned to Maine with Chamberlain and took residency in a Brunswick stable. General Chamberlain's children adopted Charlemagne as a pet. Charlemagne moved with the family when the Chamberlains established their seaside summer home – Domhegan. In the end, the beloved war steed and family pet was buried on the property. Charlemagne has been featured in a few paintings and is "immortalized" in a tapestry that hangs in the Chamberlain house.

THE PROFFERED WREATH
Gen. Chamberlain's battle-weary horse shies away from the offering of a victory wreath. May 23, 1865.

Clifton

One of the best -bred Morgans that saw service in the war was Clifton, foaled at Walpole, New Hampshire. He was by a stallion in the Woobury line and out of a mare in the Sherman line - my line! At the beginning of the Civil War, Clifton was apparently sold by F.H. Lyford to William R Capehart of North Carolina. Capehart was attending medical school in Virginia at the start of the Civil War. He enlisted in General Robert E. Lee's Army of Northern Virginia of the confederate forces as a surgeon. He was attached to Wade Hampton's cavalry. Like many of the Morgan horses who served in the Civil War, the noble animal met a war-horse's death in a cavalry engagement in 1864.

More people started moving west after the War. Many horses were lost in the Civil War and many of he Morgans that were left went with the settlers to the West. Some Vermonters became concerned about the possible depletion of their breeding stock.

Honest Allen born 1855

Today there are only two surviving sire lines from Ethan Allen and one of them is my relative, Honest Allen. Honest Allen was born in 1855 in Manchester, New Hampshire. He was a chestnut with a blaze and right front and left hind stockings and a right hind white coronet. He was 14.3 hands and weighed 950 pounds. The Honest Allen line is responsible for all the Government bred Morgans tracing through General Gates who was bred by Joseph Battell and chosen as foundation stallion for the U.S. Government Morgan Horse Farm.

The breed was growing in numbers and popularity. But it was not really a "breed" yet and could be in danger of just fizzling out. If not for the work of Daniel Linsley and Joseph Battell, it's hard to say what might have happened to the Morgan horse.

Joseph Battell was a fortunate man, with a supportive family and loyal friends. His uncle Robbins Battell was a successful manufacturer of church bells and a breeder of Morgan horses. His uncle Joseph Battell (his namesake), was a wealthy iron merchant and bachelor and at his death in 1874, established a trust fund that netted his nephew $19,000 annually (equivalent to $400,000 today). The first instilled his love for the Morgan breed, the second enabled him to fund his passions.

Battell had a passion for the natural world. He had what they called back then "weak lungs," He spent a weekend at a farmhouse in nearby Ripton, Vermont and was so taken with the beauty of the surrounding hills that he soon bought the property. The Breadloaf Inn, as he named it, grew steadily He eventually owned over 34,000 acres.

Breadloaf Inn then and now

After a promising start, the Morgan horse had begun to slide into obscurity The breed's foundation sire Figure had died in 1821. He had bred horses across Vermont and several of his sons were beginning to put their stamp on the horse-breeding world. Clearly, a type was developing; but when does a breeding type become a breed? Remember that in the Middle Ages there were types of horses - not breeds of horses. OH NO!!!! Was the Morgan horse about to just become a type instead of a breed?

Joseph Battell (1839-1915)

When Joseph Battell feared that the state's famed Morgan horses would disappear he began breeding horses in 1875 and bred nearly 150 of them during the next 40 years of his life. In 1878, he commissioned architect Clinton Smith to build a barn on land he had purchased in Weybridge.

Joseph Battell with a Morgan horse

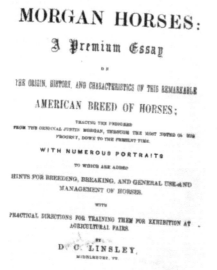

Daniel Linsley, a businessman and Middlebury, Vermont native, published *Morgan Horses: A Premium Essay on the Origin, History, and Characteristics of the Remarkable American Breed of Horses* in 1857 after several years of research and correspondence. Linsley's book began with an attempt to describe, in minute detail, a perfect type of horse, and then proceeded to inform its reader that the Morgan horse fit his defined characteristics perfectly. He recounted, as best he could, the history of Justin Morgan and his horse Figure and traced the most prominent sons of Figure. Soon after purchasing his farm, Joseph Battell began to embark on an ambitious project. He picked up Daniel Linsley's work and took it further. He retraced Linsley's steps in researching the life of Figure and added his own new efforts to that story. After nine years, during which he sent out more than 100,000 letters of inquiry and spent more than $150,000 of his own money, he published the first volume of *The Morgan Horse and Register* in 1894. It was not simply a record of a breed register but also had rules of admission and standards. Subsequent volumes followed in 1905 and, after his death, in 1915.

Battell's ideal Morgan was athletic, thrifty and keen. He particularly liked his Morgans to be fast. He preferred to drive them and would often pick up visitors to his Breadloaf Inn himself, covering the flatter miles from Middlebury to the base of the mountains at breathtaking speed. Battell admired a Morgan named Lord Clinton who had twenty race victories to his credit and a race record of 2:08 which no stallion or gelding had ever beaten. Battell hoped to buy Lord Clinton, but was unable to so, he traveled to Arkansas where he managed instead to purchase Lord Clinton's dam,

Denning Allen born 1874

Fanny Scott and sire, Denning Allen, who was by Honest Allen. Battell exhibited Denning Allen at quite a number of fairs winning First Premiums at all of them, including the 1893 World's Fair at Chicago where he was awarded First Premium for Morgan Stallions age five and older. Denning Allen was also selected by the noted German sculptor Max Landsberg to take models of some of the horses at the World's Fair for use by the agricultural schools of Germany. The cross of Denning Allen and Fanny Scott produced for Battell a magnificent horse named General Gates.

General Gates was said to closely resemble Black Hawk in type, form and color, being black with no white markings and of similar size. He proved to be an excellent sire, producing one hundred eighteen registered foals. General Gates was the foundation sire of the U.S. Morgan Horse Farm that supplied the United States with the legendary remount horses.

General Gates born 1894

Does this barn look familiar? It's the one on the cover! It's Joseph Battell's farm in Weybridge -The statue of Justin Morgan was dedicated in 1921

In May 1907, Battell offered the farm he had built to the United States government for a grand total of $1.00. The gift included the farm buildings and four hundred acres of land around the farm as well as twenty or so of his remaining horses, including General Gates, who was to become the foundation stallion of the new government breeding program. As mechanized vehicles replaced horses, the U.S. Department of Agriculture eventually concluded their cavalry remount program at the Morgan Horse Farm. The Weybridge Morgan herd was auctioned to several Land Grant Universities, including University of Connecticut and the University of Vermont. In 1951 the Weybridge property was offered to the University of Vermont, which continues to own it today and operates as the UVM Morgan Horse Farm.

Since the farm's concern was to supply the Calvary with horses between 15 and 16 hands, who were sound and substantial, they ignored the criticism directed at their foundation sire because his dam was not a purebred Morgan. The government breeding experts felt General Gates would provide a proper genetic base for the herd. The stallion proved his prepotency and by 1920, the average government-bred Morgan was 15.2 hands and 1,200 pounds. The Government Farm also instituted a testing process to ensure that only the best stock was used for breeding. This included jumping as well as a three hundred mile endurance ride in which horses were expected to finish in a maximum of five days and stay sound. The horses that were successful in the testing passed on their good conformation and fluid gaits as well as their stamina, versatility and good disposition. The long line of champions in the ring, on the trail and field and in harness bear witness to the success of this program.

Bennington born 1908

Bennington, a son of General Gates, took the place as the primary stallion at the farm in 1925. He went on to sire many of the most famous of the Government Morgans. Bennington is in the pedigrees of two thirds of the Morgans alive today - including me! The cross of Bennington to Artemisia, a chestnut mare of old Vermont breeding, produced what many called the "golden cross".

Ulysses was a product of the "golden cross"; brown with a blaze with white hind socks and white, right front foot. he was 15.3 and weighed 1,175 pounds. He produced seventeen colts and nine fillies. From 1942 to 1944 he was at the remount station in Snowmass, Colorado .

Ulysses born 1927

Ulendon born 1933

Ulendon was a son of Ulysses. He was the property of the Orcutt family for almost his entire life. My humans actually met his owner! Ulendon was not only a show horse and breeding stallion, but also a family pet. Ulendon sired fifty four of his ninety four foals after age twenty three!. Ulendon's offspring set tremendous records in the breed. He had 20.5% Justin Morgan, blood with three hundred twenty crosses back to Justin Morgan.

One of Ulendon's sons was Orcland Vigildon. He was a dark chestnut with a star and strip and white feet. He sired: fifty two colts, and fifty four fillies. He was a very fancy, high stepping horse.

Orcland Vigildon born 1947

Vigilmarch born 1957

Vigilmarch was a product of the finest bloodlines: three quarters old government and one quarter Lippitt. He passed on the characteristics he was known for: a great heart, beauty of body and soul, true athletic ability, strength and soundness. He was bred to be a performance horse and a sire of performance horses. Herbert Kohler (who had gone to a dispersal sale to purchase saddle horses for his children) bought the magnificent thirteen-year-old stallion that would cause Kohler Stables to become known as "The Vigilmarch Stud". It was at Kohler's in Wisconsin that Vigilmarch sired some of his most famous get. He produced outstanding show horses and exceptional breeding stock.

This is my grandsire, HVK Fieldmarch; born in 1975, he was the breeding son of Vigilmarch to be retained by Kohler Stables. He was a liver chestnut with a small star and white on the inside and rear of left hind coronet. WOW! just like me!!! He sired thirty four colts and forty five fillies. He was the World Champion three Year Old Park Harness Horse, Reserve World Champion three Year Old Stallion and Reserve World Champion three Year Old Park Saddle Horse.

His son, DPR Bandstand, is my sire. He was born in 1991.

Before I tell you more about my sire I need to tell you about some of the dams in my pedigree too. This is the pedigree of my dam, Foxglenns Charity. I put it sideways so you can read it. Do you see a lot of the same names?? She is impeccably bred just like my sire line is!

FOXGLENNS CHARITY
ch 15.1 hands 1980
MORGAN

Parents	Grandparents	Great-grandparents	4th gen	5th gen
BILLY BENNFIELD ch 1965 MORGAN br. by Deane Avery	BENNFIELD" b 1942 MORGAN AMHA #9940	CANFIELD" ch 1932 MORGAN AMHA #7788	BENNINGTON" b 15.1 1908	GENERAL GATES" — blk 14.3 1894 MRS CULVERS" — b 15.2 1895
			ARTEMISIA" dk ch 1909	ETHAN ALLEN 3RD" — dk ch 1885 LADY LAURA — dk 14.2 1900
		WALLFLOWER b 1929 MORGAN AMHA #04621	BENNINGTON" b 15.1 1908	GENERAL GATES" — blk 14.3 1894 MRS CULVERS" — b 15.2 1895
			QUENELDA b 1923	TROUBADOUR OF WILLOWMOOR" — b 15.2 1910 SUNFLOWER MAID" — b 1910
	RENA" ch 1947 MORGAN AMHA #07229	MAGELLAN" dk ch 1942 MORGAN AMHA #9625	GOLDFIELD" dk ch 1936	MANSFIELD" — ch 15.1 1920 JUNO" — b 1916
			TOPAZ" ch 1926	MANSFIELD" — ch 15.1 1920 LADY LYNDON — b 1910
		NUBIA" b 1943 MORGAN AMHA #06100	HUDSON" ch 1937	ADMIRAL DENMARK — b 1932 REDFERN" — ch 1924
			FAIRYTOP" b 1935	DELMONT" — b 15.1 1932 TOPAZ" — ch 1926
FIGURES DEBUTANTE dk ch 1971 MORGAN Bred by William Brown	CHASLEY SUPERMAN" dk ch 1958 MORGAN AMHA #12194	ORCLAND LEADER" ch 1944 MORGAN AMHA #9038	ULENDON" br 14.3 1933	ULYSSES" — br 15.3 1927 ALLENDA" — ch 1919
			VIGILDA BURKLAND" ch 1935	VIGILANT" — ch 1918 LUCINNE — ch 1918
		RENA" ch 1947 MORGAN AMHA #07229	MAGELLAN" dk ch 1942	GOLDFIELD" — dk ch 1936 TOPAZ" — ch 1926
			NUBIA" b 1943	HUDSON" — ch 1937 FAIRYTOP — b 1935
	OAKWOODS CHARM" dk ch 15.0 1964 MORGAN AMHA #013672	SARACEN" ch 1945 MORGAN AMHA #9615	UPWEY KING BENN" b 1939	UPWEY KING PEAVINE" — ch 15.1 1932 AUDREY" — br 1930
			ARISSA b 1930	MANSFIELD" — ch 15.1 1920 NARISSA" — b 1920
		BAR-T TWINKLE" ch 1952 MORGAN AMHA #08595	ORCLAND LEADER" ch 1944	ULENDON" — br 14.3 1933 VIGILDA BURKLAND" — ch 1935
			LADY FIELD" dk ch 1934	MANSFIELD" — ch 15.1 1920 LITTLE TROUB — b 1924

Artemisia born 1909

You need to meet some of the very famous mares in my pedigree too. I already told you a little bit about Artemisia. She was the dam that produced the "golden cross" with Bennington. She had ten foals by Bennington that became some of the most influential Morgans in the entire government program. Of the five hundred thirty three Morgans bred at the Government Farm up to the 1951 dispersal, three hundred forty three (65 percent) descended from Artemisia through her sons and daughters. She was a mare whose outstanding offspring in turn produced outstanding offspring.

Narissa is another famous mare in my pedigree. She had twenty three crosses to Sherman, thirteen crosses to Woodbury and four crosses to Bulrush. Here is a picture of her with one of her seventeen foals, Dimity, born in 1933. The importance of Narissa cannot be overstated. She founded a large and prolific family, the members of which have been used by breeders across the country.

Narissa born 1920

The list of breeders who used her produce and the next generations beyond is truly a who's who of the Morgan world. Most of her produce would fill a magazine article on their own, as would many of their progeny. Many have had articles in The Morgan Horse Magazine in the past and many more will be written about in the future (like me I even had Breyer horse made of me!) She gave her produce a solid heritage of Morgan greatness, and they lived up to that. Today Narissa has descendants in Austria, Canada, France, Germany, Great Britain, Puerto Rico, Sweden and America.

Vigilda Burkland was a dark chestnut mare; she had both type and quality, as well as one of the best produce records. Her two best sons were the two full brothers by Ulendon, Orland Leader and Orland Vigildon. She had five colts and five fillies. The mares she produced were also excellent broodmares just like she was. She was 100% old Vermont breeding with ninety four crosses to Sherman, forty two crosses to Woodbury, and eleven crosses to Bulrush.

Vigilda Burkland born 1935

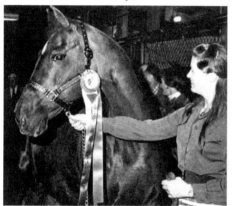

Rena born 1947

Rena was a remarkable Government-bred mare and a prolific dam of excellent offspring; she is the grand-dam of five World Champion mares. Her name is firmly established in the pedigrees of many top Morgans today. And, coolest thing of all, she could write too just like me! For a span of several years in the late 1960s and early 1970s she was responsible for capturing the minds and hearts of countless numbers of the horsey set—young and old alike. She 'talked' from page three of The Morgan Horse magazine in those days.

Foxglenns Charity born 1980

This is my dam, Foxglenns Charity. Now I need to tell you how she "met" my sire, DPR Bandstand.

CHAPTER 10 ~ My Arrival

I was born at Heart's Delight Farm. That's what the HD is in my name. All of the horses born there are named after cites in New York. Harkness, New York is in upstate New York across Lake Champlain from Burlington, Vermont. The building of Heart's Delight Farm began in 1903 and grew from a farmhouse and a couple of barns on one hundred forty four acres, into a model farm of three hundred structures situated on fifteen thousand acres. The farm utilized a scientific approach to agriculture on a vast scale, embracing hydroelectric power and technological advances to run an enterprise that employed eight hundred workers in its heyday. It shipped ham, sausages, eggs and other produce to the best hotels and restaurants in New York City and Chicago.

Heart's Delight Farm was developed on William Henry Miner's family homestead. By 1918, the farm had grown to twelve thousand acres - four thousand acres of tillable land, two thousand acres of pasture and six thousand acres of woodland. Within the cropland, four hundred fifty acres were devoted to growing corn and six hundred acres to small grains. There was a wide variety of animals on the farm including beef and dairy cattle, mules, draft horses, purebred horses, sheep, pigs, chickens, turkeys, pheasants and brook trout. The farm had its own dairy, box factory, ice house, natatorium, greenhouses and grist mill. There was a twenty bedroom guesthouse and an entertainment center named Harmony Hall, which included an auditorium, complete with a stage, that could accommodate 300 persons.

Development of this lovely gentleman's farm was made possible by the fortune Mr. Miner earned from his mechanical inventions for rail transportation. The farm continued to thrive during Mr. Miner's lifetime as he divided his time between the farm and his company, Miner, Inc., based in Chicago. Mr. Miner's will provided for the establishment of a school and farm devoted to teaching scientific and environmentally sound agricultural practices to the farmers and youth of northern New York.

Today the Miner Institute uses its farm, facilities, and staff to conduct fully integrated education, research, and demonstration programs on the dairy-crop interface, equine reproduction and management and environmental conservation.

Mr. Miner strongly believed in high quality education and registered live-stock, so the versatile Morgan Horse was a natural fit. Today the few foals each year registered with the Heart's Delight Farm prefix, "HD" form the core of the educational program's mission. The stables and herd are used to demonstrate good farm, breeding, and training practices. Miner Institute maintains a herd of Morgan Horses as the core of the educational program. All horses owned by the Institute are donated, home bred, or the result of a donated stallion service. *(Read more about the Moner Institute here https://www. whminer.org/)*

And that is how I came to be. My sire, DPR Bandstand was at the farm providing donated stallion services to the mares owned by the Miner Institute as well as mares brought in by private owners. My dam was one of the mares owned by the Miner Institute. The picture above is how the Miner Institute horse barn looks today and here is one of me as a weanling in the

pasture there. Miner's has created some great horses - me included of course! My first owner, Dawn, saw me in the field as a weanling when she had her mare there to breed to my sire. She said I was perfect for her breeding program so she purchased me right away. She says I was a sheer delight to work with.

Dawn was on vacation one week during my yearling summer, when her caretaker turned me out with the whole herd, including my half sister. Well boys will be boys and six months later it became obvious that my half sister was in foal - oops! Shortly after that Dawn had a back injury which curtailed her plans about standing a stud so she needed to part with me. Miner Institute helped her advertise me and that's when my current owners

VQ Adirondack Revolution

found me. They brought their family to meet me and guess what happened the day before they met me - my son, VQ Adirondack Revolution was born.

It was a very hectic day when my "to be" family arrived and Dawn did not have a chance to groom me or work me before my new owners showed up with their children. She lunged me a little before handing me over to this new person who wanted me. It was within those few first moments, that I chose my new human. It was so obvious to Dawn that I had a connection already. This was one sale Dawn said she didn't question. Deal made. My new family went for a little vacation in Montreal. Dawn's intentions were to work with me loading on a horse trailer before they took me home, since I had only been on the trailer twice as a yearling, but her injured back was just not up to it. Fortunately though, Miner's had done trailer work with me as a weanling and I'm smart so I remembered those lessons and I hopped right on the trailer. And thus the new adventures for me started. Twenty three years later and I'm still with the same family!!! Dawn has always said that to know a beloved horse goes to a new owner and remains there his entire life is a huge gift and she is glad that she got to play a part in me finding my life people!

It was about a ten hour drive to my new home. Our journey foretold the type of horse I would become: stoic, brave, energetic and faithfully trustworthy.

On the way home from New York, we were stuck on a bridge in Toronto during a tornado warning. The horse trailer rocked terribly in the wind and my humans feared that I would panic and get injured and probably never want to get in a trailer again. But when they checked on me, I was quietly and happily munching hay. No storm was going to keep me from enjoying a road trip to some awesome new adventure! My new family knew right then that I was the perfect choice; but they really already knew that even before they met me.

In July of 2000 they were looking for a young Morgan horse to add to their little herd of three other Morgans. This was before YouTube, Facebook and websites so they contacted owners and breeders throughout the US and Canada and had them send VHS videos of their sale horses. Oh what beautiful horses they enjoyed watching on those videos! It was a hard decision but my humans were leaning toward a lovely two year old bay stallion. So they gathered a group of friends and had a Video Viewing Party – with carrot cake of course! After the viewing, everyone was to vote by secret ballot. The decision was unanimous – it was decided that the lovely two year old bay stallion - ME!!! - would become a member of their family. Here are pictures of me the day I got to my new home.

CHAPTER 11 ~ Happily Ever After

Some horses find their forever home when they are very young - I did. I am twenty five now and I have been with the same family since that day I joined them when I was two. They taught me to drive and ride. I learned words like "trot", "walk", "canter" and "whoa" and funny noises that sound like tick tock on a clock. I've traveled to so many places; Kentucky, Wisconsin, New York, Canada and more. I've been to schools, parades and horse expos. One summer lots of places were closed so everyone in the country had to stay home. My humans nieces did not get to go to horse camp so I was the horse they spent the summer with; I like it when I can make people happy. I've met new humans and had new adventures every place I went. I'll tell you about a few of my adventures.

The first thing I leaned was how to lunge. Lunging is when a horse is on a long line that is held by a person and the horse works around the person in a circle. The person holds a long whip to encourage the horse to move forward. The purpose for lunging is for the horse to gain strength, confidence and obedience. This is when I learned words like "walk", "trot", "canter" and "whoa". Lunging also helped me to learn my human's body language - when she stopped I learned to stop. When she walked, I would walk. It was a great time for us to get to know each other.

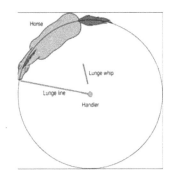

I'm so good at lunging now that sometimes I get excited on the end of a lunge line when I get to a new place just to get out some of my energy - and to let everyone watching know that I have some pretty amazing moves!

Next I had to learn how to long line. It's kind of like lunging but this is when I got to be like the big guys and wear a bridle with a bit. Since I already knew what words meant, now my human could ask me to do those things on command - like "walk" - what a surprise when I moved forward and felt a little pressure on the bit in my mouth! I'm pretty smart so it did not take long for me to reach right into the bit and turn when I felt just the slightest pressure on one side or another. I'm really, really good at long lining now! My human has given demonstrations and lessons with me to help people learn how to long line.

After I learned all of that, it was time to learn how to pull a carriage. I caught on to that super fast. Like in one day! I think that's because I'm smart and very athletic. Plus I take a lot of joy in making people happy. That's kind of Morgan horse thing. The Morgan is known as "the horse that chooses you". Morgans love people and want to make them happy. I am the absolute personification of a Morgan! "A friendly horse that is typically quite eager to please its handlers and even enjoys meeting strangers. Although it can be animated and spunky, it's still very affectionate and known for its loyalty." *(cited from: https://www.thesprucepets.com/morgan-horse-breed-profile-1886128)* Yup - that's me!

Here are some pictures of me driving.

This is me at home with my carriage called a Flyer. It's newly made and good for cross country and schooling.

The Flyer is great for going cross country too. I like it when I get to go fast!

Sometimes I even get to use it at horse shows.

I have a road cart too. It was made in about 1920. I like to use it when I'm going casual. Like the Flyer, it's great for training at home, doing obstacles and just zooming around.

Sometimes I use it at shows too

Here is another carriage that I get to use. It's called a Concord Wagon and it was built in 1872. It's the kind of carriage you would see in the old Currier and Ives prints with a Morgan horse so it's perfect for me!

The carriage is all original except for new carpeting, new shafts and new fabric on the parasol. The body of the carriage is patterned after the curved body of the Concord Stagecoaches. When traveling, the curved body allowed cargo to shift toward the middle of the vehicle rather than bounce out. How smart of the people who designed this very utilitarian carriage. This wagon also has a triple perch similar to the Concord Stagecoaches. It has a torsion suspension which was later used in automobiles. The side-bar and cross-spring gear on this carriage were introduced about 1870; in response to demands of speed, drivers wanted a more stable vehicle than the end-spring or elliptic variety provided. The high wheels of almost equal size were used to reduce the resistance on rough surfaces - but they greatly reduced the turning ability of the vehicle. The wheels are on the original iron rather than rubber.

Behind a fast, high-spirited horse, like me, a driver could make quite an impression driving this flashy model. Made of birds eye maple, it has etched glass lamps and other unique features such as a parasol to be used when driven by a lady.

I've won lots of ribbons when I am put to this carriage. I think I look very handsome with it!

The Carriage Association of America even used my picture with this carriage to advertise their horse show!

I often get put to a formal carriage too. This carriage is called a Wicker Phaeton. It was built in 1903 by Locke and Company of New York. Locke later went on to build car bodies for Cadillac, Duesenberg, Mercedes, Packard, Pierce-Arrow, Renault, Rolls-Royce and others.

As ladies began to drive, this design appealed to them because of the ease of getting in and out and the fact that their dresses could be seen. After a time, carriages of this design-type were often referred to as Ladies Phaetons. Some with wicker bodies were intended for summer use and the folding parasol top could be added to provide protection from the sun.

Before my family bought this carriage it was owned by Jimmy Cagney; he was a very well known actor; he made sixty two movies and even won an Oscar! He also bred Morgan horses on his farm in New York. Here is a picture of him and one of him driving our carriage on his farm in New York with his Morgans.

I look pretty fancy with this carriage - I think I could win an Oscar too! My humans love driving it because they say it rides like a luxury car. They also like it because they can take passengers too and have picnics - and even our dog rides along sometimes!

Getting ready to go to a show means I get extra pampering! I love getting baths and grooming is like a massage! When I get to the show, I even get a fan on my stall. I relax while I watch my humans work hard cleaning tack and carriages and loving on our dog who gets to come too.

Here I am getting ready for a bath and eating grass while I dry after my bath

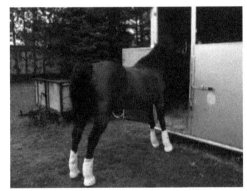

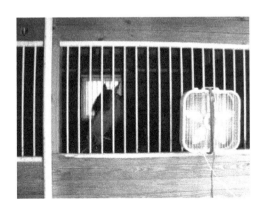

I'm versatile too - like most Morgans. When I was four years old, my human started riding me. She says I am "bomb proof" and fun to ride.

She really likes taking pictures of me because I make the tress look good.

And I look pretty good when I get dressed up for a show too - even without a carriage behind me!

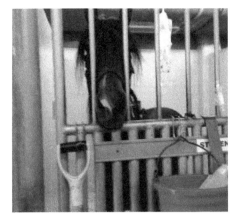

I got sick once and had to go to a veterinary clinic. They said I was a good patient but, as much as I like going on adventures, I was still glad to get home.

Sometimes my adventures are as simple as going for a hand-walk. My humans call it "bonding" time and they talk to me a lot while we are walking.

I was part of the parade unit for our Morgan Horse Club too. I had to go through mounted police training to be able to be allowed into the unit and I passed on the very first day - yup - because I AM bomb proof! I played the part of Figure with his owner Justin Morgan (my human) and lead all of the other horses. After all, I do look a lot like Figure!

I like meeting new people too - especially students at schools because they write the best thank you notes!!!

Thank you for showing us your horse. They were very beautiful

Thank you for showing us your horse. I think Figure is my favorite because he is soft and nice.

My humans have other horses too and I enjoy hanging out with them -as long as they remember that I am in charge.

But I have to keep an eye on everything when they pay attention to the other horses and not me because you never know when those other horses will need to learn a few things from me!

I can't wait to tell you more about horses! I have a blog on a web site (www.hoofbeatsthroughhistory.com) and I have other books too. I am looking forward to spending time with you again soon - but for now, I think I'll take a nap.

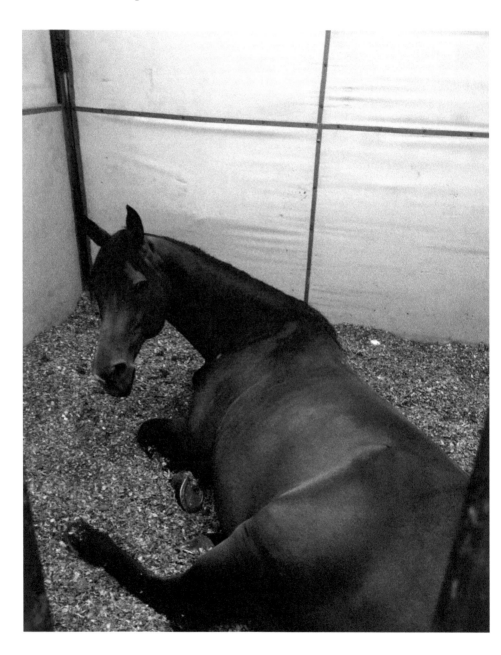

FURTHER READING TO LEARN MORE

To learn more about Morgan horses, visit some of these links.

http://www.eyewitnesstohistory.com/nationalroad.htm

https://www.morganhorse.com/upload/photos/904BlackHawk1.14.pdf

https://www.morganhorse.com/upload/photos/245History.pdf

https://www.morganhorse.com/upload/photos/206RESEARCHTrottingCousins2010.pdf

https://sites.middlebury.edu/breadloaf/joseph-battell/

https://vermonthistory.org/documents/VermontMagazine/29_1_MarchApril2017Morgan-Horse.pdf

https://www.burlingtonfreepress.com/story/news/local/2015/06/05/hoofprints-history-weybridge/28504085/

https://civilwartalk.com/threads/pink-col-john-hammonds-morgan-horse.135775/

http://morganhorseguide.com/2016/03/10/morgan-horses-in-the-civil-war/

https://dotcw.com/col-sharpes-horses/ https://gazette665.com/2017/01/13/chamberlains-charlemagne/comment-page-1/

http://morganhorseguide.com/2016/03/10/old-abe-and-clem-famous-morgan-horses-of-the-civil-war/

https://www.civilwarprofiles.com/traveller-and-little-sorrel-the-war-horses-of-lee-and-jackson/

https://www.americancivilwarforum.com/the-black-horse-troop-2184825.html

http://morganhorseguide.com/tag/famous-morgan-horses/

https://www.morganhorse.com/upload/photos/1078TMHBloodWillTell_Bennington_JuneJuly2017.pdf

https://www.morganhorse.com/magazine/archive-articles/blood-will-tell/

https://animalscience.cahnr.uconn.edu/wp-content/uploads/sites/3396/2022/04/index_16_4219819196.pdf

https://www.morganhorse.com/magazine/archive-articles/blood-will-tell/

https://www.morganhorse.com/upload/photos/1078TMHBloodWillTell_Vigilmarch_NovDec2013.pdf

https://www.morganhorse.com/upload/photos/page_904_tmh_nov_dec2020_people_june_brockett_wright.pdf

https://www.morganhorse.com/upload/photos/1078TMHBloodWillTell_Rena_March2018.pdf

https://www.morganhorse.com/upload/photos/1078TMHBloodWillTell_Artemisia_April2014.pdf

https://www.morganhorse.com/upload/photos/1078TMHBloodWillTell_Narissa_Sept2016.pdf

https://www.whminer.org/

Ingram Content Group UK Ltd.
Milton Keynes UK
UKHW050840240523
422259UK00009B/62